NOWHEREMAG.COM

Viñales, Cuba

Pacifica, California

Nizhny Tagil, Russia

Cadaqués, Spain

IMAGES:

2–3	Doug Despres
4–5	Arthur Kobin
6–7	Spencer Wohlrab
8–9	Sara Fox

NOWHERE

TRAVEL STORIES

2019

Onion Flavored Rings

TX-SF

BY MICHAEL BOUSHEE

FIREWORKS, WARRANTS, CHICKEN BARBECUES, GOLDEN BULLETS, CRAIGSLIST, BUBBLE COATS, DEAD BODIES, ROLL-YOUR-OWNS, THE BAY, BREAKDOWNS, BURIED WEED, SOCAL LOSERS & AUSTIN.

We had to get the fuck out of Texas. Besides getting kicked out of the apartment we piled up in, most of us had warrants out for our arrest and we had just spent the last of our collective money bailing Luke out of jail.

It seemed every hasher from the cold and frozen Northeast landed unemployed in Austin that winter, looking for a nut. No one worked. Some people had food stamps to support chicken barbecues in the dusty backyard of the Comal house, where Drew rented a room. We began camping outside a cave in the Greenbelt. I spent the hot days kicking rocks around the sidewalk, hoping for something to change.

At the library with a guest pass, I signed on to Craigslist, searching for a come-up.

"Drive my bus from TX to SF," the ad read. I responded and

a reply came from Robinsong: "Pick up the keys from my friend. Save receipts. Drive to San Rafael. I'll send you money."

Sparkling, sundrenched images of a plush hippie bus and beautiful women roped in smoke flurried through my imagination.

We talked on the phone. I faxed a photocopy of my ID and picked up $400 at the Fiesta Mart Western Union. In a full-sized orange cheese-wagon, we rolled up to the front porch on Comal Street. People piled on, some who were planning on it and others who couldn't say no. We managed our way onto the highway and took a left out of Texas.

We drove and drove and drove, stopping only for gas. Long shadows of mountains and mesas stretched out in front of us and shrunk as the sun climbed higher, as the day got on. The windows caked in icy frost then thawed like hot breath while descending from New Mexico to Arizona's Painted Desert.

The bus broke down in the Petrified Forest in sweltering heat. Riders climbed on and off and kept busy reading, rolling cigs and drawing in Sharpie, covering the white ceiling to the rivets.

When we finally broke through to the Pacific, we ran in the sand at the base of towering cliffs. I felt tiny like a mouse and jumped in and out of the freezing-cold water. We drove up the 101 along sheer rock faces, past beaches studded with packs of elephant seals, and shot fireworks off the pier in Santa Monica.

By the time the radiator blew in San Luis Obispo, we were ready to get rid of the bus. I called all the numbers I had until finally a guy answered, said he was Robinsong's boyfriend and told us where to go.

The fantasy hippie babes we had imagined turned out to be a handful of bona fide SoCal losers. No money or jobs—one asked if Connecticut was in Delaware. The one with spiky gelled hair and a bubble coat told us in hushed baby tones that they "don't have money, but have...stuff...acid, mushrooms, weed..."

Tyler was along for the ride seeing the country for the first time and had put up everything my meager unemployment check didn't cover. His stutter kept him from joining the military the way he wanted, and he wasn't interested in "stuff."

Weed seemed the most marketable. A college kid was fixing a dryer on the street when a dumpy truck pulled up and I saw those gelly spikes glinting like glass. He stuffed a freezer bag full of weed under John's arm and said, "Don't be shady!"

We beelined for the tracks to smoke a cig and strategize. A trimmer friend in the Bay thought they could help us peddle the stuff if we came and stayed with them. So we bused up to Oakland. The first thing I found walking on the sidewalk in West Oakland was a tiny gold bullet. Kids banged on the trash cans and sang "Fuck the Police."

We waited on the corner, doing our best to look regular, until we dipped one by one behind a sheet of plywood into a dilapidated old house, where Carl and Ashley were squatting. The place was caving in and the walls were draped in mold. We pissed in the back and shat in a hole in the floor.

Carl and Ashley had a street-rat swag that got us in and out of trouble from Oakland to San Francisco and back every day for as long as it took to pay back Tyler. We stayed with them until a dead body was pulled out of the back yard.

On our last night in the Bay together, John and I slept behind the bushes in the Safeway parking lot. I still had a decent chunk of weed left, so I buried it in a Funyuns bag, in case anyone bothered us. Months later, once I was back on the East Coast, Carl called asking which bush I had buried it under. I described it to him and he dug it up and sold what was left.

MICHAEL BOUSHEE *lives in Woodstock, New York, where he works as a gardener and occasionally writes.*

SO MANY STORIES

BY MARJORY WOODFIELD

MARESHAS, ROCK-HEWN CHURCHES, AXUM, SAINT GEORGE'S HORSE, BONFIRES, PAPYRUS BOATS, NOAH'S ARK, BUNA, *CHANTING ROOMS, TEFF, WATERFALLS, MESKEL, GOOD HARVESTS, FOSSILS & THE FESTIVAL OF THE FINDING OF THE TRUE CROSS.*

THROUGH THE DARKNESS

Nine hundred years ago, King Lalibela had a dream. God told him to build a new Jerusalem for Ethiopia's Christians. Pilgrimage to the real Jerusalem was impossible, because it was under Muslim control. Lalibela did. Eleven great rock-hewn monolithic and semi-monolithic churches, carved into and under a cumin-coloured landscape. Invisible. Excavated from the top down and the inside out. Solid stone, connected by a labyrinth of underground passages. Construction was rapid because God's angels picked up the stonemasons' chisels each night, carried on working through the darkness. We cross the small, muddy creek that Lalibela named the Jordan River. Earthly city on one side, celestial Jerusalem on the other. Walk to the House of Saint George, Biet Gyorgis. Our guide tells us it represents Noah's Ark, points to the lower-level windows, which are sealed, and says, "Because it has to be watertight." Behind the church a rocky mound signifies Mount Ararat, and a recessed pool, the water that carried the Ark. We hear another story. Saint George appeared on his white horse as workers completed the tenth church. "Where is *my* church?" he asked. "Yours will be next and it will be the last and the finest," he was told. As we turn to leave, I see cup-shaped indentations on a wall, hoof prints of Saint George's horse.

CHAINS AND FIRE

We cross Lake Tana to the island monasteries of Bahir Dar. Pass traditional fishermen in papyrus boats, a pair of half-submerged hippos and a flock of white pelicans. The morning is low cloud. Distant cliffs slip into water. Follow a muddy track to the circular monastery of Ura Kidane Mihret. In the chanting room there are drums against walls. Mary, the mother, holds Jesus. She is draped in fabric the colour of lapis lazuli, dotted with stars. The Egyptians sink in the Red Sea beside Pharaoh. Moses, safely on higher ground. Beside a camel, a merchant holds a needle, the eye clearly visible. The devil consumes the wicked. Chains and fire. Saint George slays the dragon, and on the ceiling, disciples fish on calm Galilee waters. We walk to a small museum beside the church. The priest brings out an ancient manuscript. Saint Yared, taking the voices of three birds, their intermingled song, creating a system of music still in use. His picture on one side of the page. Music on the other.

ALL DIRECTIONS

Along the road to Gondar, women walk to market bowed under bundles of vegetables and grain. Men, barefooted, shoulders draped with white cotton shawls, carry a figure on a wooden stretcher to a health clinic. Our SUV vies with donkeys for space on the potholed road. We pass fields of teff, wheat, chickpeas. See farmers tilling the earth with traditional wooden ploughs, pulled by oxen and mules. Mareshas. When there's a brief stop to check a tyre, children run through fields from all directions to see us. A collection of *tukul* huts, goats, chickens, washing on makeshift lines. Adeba stands in her doorway. A red scarf twists 'round her head. Orange plastic bucket on the ground. She scoops a cupful of batter, pours it onto a hot plate. Bends, adjusting the logs, then waits. Eyes full of smoke. Edges a paper-thin *injera* off the plate. One more to go on the pile to sell later at the market. She smiles, hands me the cup, points to the orange bucket.

IN THE DUST

"So, do you like your African massage?" I nod to the back of Tassew's head. He continues driving and we hit another pothole. Limalimo Road, from the Simien Mountains to Axum. "There's a story about this road," he says. "Once Haile Selassie was travelling here. But then he said to his driver, "Stop, I want to get out and walk. I like walking." He pauses to laugh. "But really, he was frightened." I look through the window at the steepness of our descent, the closeness of the edge and sheer drop. We pass a waterfall on our right and stop for a photograph because it reminds us of home. Further on we spot a vervet monkey. It's small, gray-faced and moves too quickly for a photo. We bump our way down the twisting road. An Abyssinian rose flowers in the dust. Distant mountains are yellow with meskel flowers.

RITUAL

In Axum the market is dusty. Women sit cross-legged on the ground, braid garlic. Spices spill out of hemp sacks. Lentils, teff, mustard seed, barley, powdered chili and berbere. Small girls carry babies on their backs. Camels, cows, goats and sheep wander freely. A wooden cart followed by a blue tuk-tuk cuts through the crowd. "Blue virus," mutters Tassew as we jump aside. A young boy and girl pass holding live chickens, strung upside down and squawking. I try to count, but they move too quickly. One shop sells brightly coloured plastic sandals. Outside, a young boy threads a needle with red cotton, ready to mend a large umbrella open on his lap. Yordanos is nine. She's in charge of her father's carpentry shop. She points to a row of bedheads and says the price, speaking in Amharic to Tassew. He laughs and says at that price she needs to also include breakfast. We walk to the women's basket market. The colours are bold, designs geometric. *Sefaed*: a large flat basket for cleaning grain. *Mesob*: a wide basket with a tapering pedestal used for serving injera. One minute they are neat rows. The next, three goats appear from nowhere, trampling, scattering, disappearing. We sit in front of Samara, under an old fig tree. Her son waits a short distance away. She's just dragged him away from fighting with a friend, cuffing him around the ears. Now he's close enough to his mother so she can keep an eye on him. Not so close that he'll receive any more unwanted attention. She begins the ritual of preparing coffee, *buna*. 1. Over a small charcoal burner, raw coffee beans roast in a flat iron pan. 2. Samara fans the aroma in our direction. 3. The roasted beans are crushed into a fine powder with mortar and pestle. 4. The powder is put into a traditional earthenware coffee pot, *jebena*, with boiling water. 5. Frankincense is lit. The smoke carries away bad spirits and cleans the air. 6. Samara arranges small cups close together on a tray. 7. She pours the coffee in a single stream from about a foot above the cups, filling each one without breaking the flow. Hands us the cups.

MOST WAITED FOR

Meskel in Adigrat. So far north we can almost see Eritrea in the distance. Meskel is the Festival of the Finding of the True Cross. It's also the name given to small yellow daisies that appear every spring. Centuries ago, Queen Helena in Jerusalem heard God's voice in a dream, lit a bonfire. The smoke led her to the cross of Christ. A remnant was brought back to Ethiopia for the Christians there. Nowadays, it's protected by monks in Gishen Mariam Monastery, on the high, flat-topped mountain of Amba Geshen. We enter Adigrat's stadium and see the bonfire. Demera. At the top, a cross and meskel flowers. Deacons and bishops wear bright ceremonial robes, hold fringed umbrellas. Gold jeweled crosses. In the distance small boys jump, clap and laugh as they wait to parade. A brass band processes around the stadium. We find a shady place in the food tent beside piles of injera. A woman pokes at logs underneath a bubbling pot of *tihlo*. In another tent women make the barley dough balls that will be added later. We're offered buna and sit with the small cups of black coffee, watching. A horse crops grass beside us. Embroidered on its coat is the Lion of Judah. The owner talks to us, says its name is Happy. A young boy approaches selling religious texts. He's wearing a long green robe and hat decorated with gold crosses. The man beside me takes one. I look over his shoulder at the unfamiliar Amharic script before he hands it back. There's dancing and singing in another part of the stadium. Bottle caps strung around the shins of dancers jingle and long hollow metal pipes resonate. The lighting of the Meskel bonfire by the Patriarch is next. It's the moment most waited for. The Patriarch descends from the stand. Cross high in the air, he walks around the bonfire. He gives a blessing, is ready to light the fire. "There's a problem," Tassew suddenly whispers in my ear. "They can't find matches." This is a non-smoking country. No matches or cigarette lighters hidden in any of these pockets. Minutes later, a young deacon comes running toward the Patriarch. The bonfire leaps into flames. The direction of the smoke and final collapse of the demera is a predictor of good harvests. Tomorrow, charcoal will be collected from the ashes and used to mark crosses on foreheads. We leave Adigrat and drive south towards Mekele. I sit with my camera on my lap, scrolling through photos, glancing out the window at passing villages. Each with its own small bonfire. Each decorated with yellow meskel daisies.

THE WEIGHING OF SOULS

In Tigray, we climb to the cave church of Abreha we Atsbeha. From outside, the sound of responsive chanting. Saint Yared's birdsong. Inside, a basket of sistrums and wooden prayer staffs propped against the doorway. Storytelling walls. Adam and Eve, the Lion of Judah, Judgment Day and the weighing of souls. Text in ancient Ge'ez. "It's about Thomas," Tassew says quietly. "He's reading the part where he says he won't believe until he sees Christ's hands and feels the spear marks." A green-robed priest takes a large hand bell and slowly shakes it backward and forward. Four clergy in an array of colours appear from the Holy of Holies. Hiding place of the Tabot, Ark of the Covenant. Scattered worshippers move forward and wait for the bread and the wine. We walk into the body of the church. Tassew says it's named after twin brothers, Abreha and Atsbeha, who ruled in the fourth century and, according to story, were the first to bring Christianity to this region. I look for Saint George and the Dragon. "He's in every church," I tell Tassew. "He must be here somewhere too." We both scan the walls, but time's up, the service is over, the last saffron-clad figure is leaving, and now the priest too is waiting to lock up. We walk to where we've left our shoes, slowly down the hill back to our car, past the children holding small fossils crying, "Only forty birr."

MARJORY WOODFIELD *is a writer and teacher of literature. She has returned to Christchurch, New Zealand, after living in Saudi Arabia for the last seven years. Her travel writing has been published by the* BBC, Stuff *(New Zealand) and various journals in Saudi Arabia.*

VERANO

BY JACK ANTAL

JACK ANTAL *is a photographer based in California. You can follow him @_captainjackk.*

GÅ FRAM

BY KELSEY CAMACHO

TUNDRA, ALASKAN HUSKIES, RAW MEAT, DISORIENTATION, GANG LINES, THE BLUE HOUR, SVALBARD, WIND SONGS, LIFELESS BATTERIES, SEA ICE, ISOLATION, REINDEER HIDES, CARMEN, MELTING MINERALS, CANINE TELEPATHY & THE COMPASS OF INSTINCT.

It was like watching the Earth being flattened, sledding into the whiteout. It was like the whole Earth was being flattened in a closing book—the kind of story you look up from with longing. The eight dogs pulling my sled looked like they were being erased, snow filling their fur. Their ears were back, tails down in concentration, and it looked like they were halfway gone. We were on our way back from an overnight trip, and we had made it to a neighboring valley, twenty kilometers from home. The mountains, the sky, the tundra: everything was lost.

Storms like this, the ones that take over Svalbard out of nowhere, move like ghosts. Sometimes I see them sneaking in from the other end of the valleys, or spilling over the glaciers, and other times it storms as if nothing else ever happens in the north. I could take my attention off the landscape for a few seconds—to check the pulling lines on the dogs, to look at my watch—and the next time I'd see the land it would be nearly invisible, swallowed by one flat shade of white-gray. The wind pushes the snow so fast that it seems like the flurries move in slow motion, a grainy tape recording and unwinding itself.

In some stretches of tundra, the wind had blown away all the snow, leaving bare sheets of ice and rock jutting from the ground. I trusted my dogs. One of the leaders, Carmen, was guiding us among the fragmented skeleton of tundra. I held tightly to the sled, shifting my weight to avoid tipping over. Like driving a dogsled on the moon. We could have been a million miles from anything.

An archipelago halfway between mainland Norway and the North Pole, Svalbard is a chain of islands that feels forgotten. How could any form of life exist in a place so lonely? There's a scale of light and darkness that never quite balances—months of night, blue hours of twilight, the sun that stays above the horizon all summer. The energy in the body sinks to hibernation in the polar night and I spend the end of winter waking. That first shock of sunlight hitting the mountaintops in a pale pink glow—the kind of color that exists in dreams. Every time I start to know this place, it shifts again; meltwater channels carve the glaciers, rivers open in the spring, snowfall shapes the land like clay. What alien world is this?

Every time I start to know myself, I shift again. Before moving to Svalbard, I had never driven dogs or lived in the Arctic. It was all easily romanticized: being a dog musher in a postcard version of winter, carefully formed snowfall and reflective light. In reality, the days were getting shorter and I didn't know anything. I had a hundred moments of waking, the hypnic jerk that startles the body before drifting asleep. That moment of opening your eyes before falling from the cliff.

There were times when I couldn't wake fast enough. I lost a team of dogs and they ran six kilometers home without me; I got my hand bitten when breaking up a fight; I fell from a sled and was dragged across ice, black bruises blooming on my knees for weeks afterward. So many times I failed, felt like I was imagining an identity I never deserved. Everything I knew about myself was suddenly wrong for where I was: I couldn't shoot a gun, or measure the thickness of sea ice, or free a truck from a snowbank. How easily we find our limitations in an unknown landscape. When the darkness came and I searched for the opposite side of the fjord outside the window, there was nothing, just my own sinking reflection.

The farther we went into the valley, the harder it was to tell if we were moving or standing still. We were in a two-dimensional space, a void between here and there. I stood on the brake and laid down the anchor so I could find the GPS inside my bag. Carmen looked back at me with confusion, as if to question my decision.

She threw herself into the snow and rolled around. The rest of the team started eating snow, panted and then tried pulling some more, jumping in place on the gang line. This is how dogs deal with being lost: they continue.

The GPS was dead, battery drained by the temperature. I was glad to have Carmen with me; she was one of the most experienced dogs in the pack. She was calm, brave and confident in her direction. Sometimes I'd watch her during bad weather and she would be stoic, looking into the storm. While all the other dogs barked and jumped and howled before running, she lay down and waited, staring ahead at whatever path we were taking.

Before Willem Barentsz discovered Svalbard in 1596, most of the Arctic was unknown. It was a white space on the map. He stumbled across it while sailing to find the Northeast Passage, which he did not. He did find Bjørnøya (Bear Island), the southernmost island on Svalbard, which he named after his battle with a polar bear upon arrival. He described the surrounding land as full of "jagged peaks" and brimming with life—whales, seals, walruses, bears and a variety of birds. According to Barentsz, the sea was filled with so many bowhead whales that ships had to break paths through them; a person could walk across the fjord on their backs.

His discovery set the pace for hundreds of years of exploration and exploitation. European ships first went north for the whale blubber; the whales were harpooned and pulled to the side of the boat, where long strips of blubber were cut off. Whaling stations were built on shore, huge copper boilers that turned the blubber into oil. When the whales eventually withdrew from the fjords, the hunt took place in the open sea and the blubber was boiled on the boats. By the end of the eighteenth century, most of the whales were gone.

I learned to live like a dog. I spent every day with the pack for months, trying to understand their language. They were eighty-five Alaskan huskies, their own complete nation. When one of the dogs was loose or injured, they all reacted instantaneously with barks and howls—even the ones on the opposite end of the yard. If other teams of dogs passed through the area, the pack was loud with claiming their space. They were connected by some invisible web, the same brainwave that alerted to anything.

The yard was in the valley, ten kilometers outside of town. Each morning I loaded the truck with boxes of raw meat and warm water so it wouldn't freeze on the drive out. I woke up during the drive on the only road leading out of town, listening to a Norwegian talk show while heat rattled from the dash.

As soon as I got close to the yard, the dogs exploded with energy; they knew the sound of the truck and that it meant food. It was heavy work, especially if it had snowed the day before, and feeding all of them sometimes took hours. There were days of crawling on two-meter-deep snow to avoid sinking down, days of digging snow out of all eighty-five houses. I grew muscles that I never knew existed. There was something relieving about being there, just me and all those dogs, nothing around us. Sometimes the wind would blow through the chain-link fence in an ethereal, drifting song.

I left work every day covered in dust, dog poop and raw meat, completely drained of physical and mental energy. I woke up, drove out to the dogs, drove home, ate and slept—a simple existence with not much room for anything else. On some days when the exhaustion bore down to the bone, I wondered how much longer I would last there. It was hard to recognize myself.

When I first started running them on the sleds, I was anxious and clumsy, always tipping over, unsure of my leaders. I couldn't find a reason to explain why I was doing any of it. A part of me liked the discomfort, the physicality of working outdoors, an observation of dog psychology rather than human.

The dogs were my motivation. They never lost energy or their will to run. It was perseverance in its truest form, and not only did they accept the harsh conditions of the environment, but they seemed to thrive in it: running headfirst into the wind, sleeping outside their houses during below-forty windchill. There was Diesel, a male built like a tank and with a childish cry; Fernet, who always wrapped his front legs around my shin in a clinging hug; Lucky, who liked collecting stones. On days in the yard when the weather was tame, they would lie on top of their houses and sleep.

I kept going out on the sled alone, experiencing problems and having no choice but to learn their solutions. Whenever something happened, which it inevitably did—a fight, broken lines, getting stuck in deep snow—I looked to my best dogs and watched how they reacted. I learned to follow their energy, and they did the same for me. We read from each other. If I was calm, they were too. There was a balance, a type of trust that wherever we were going, we would help each other get there.

Every time I went out in storms, on heavy trails, on longer trips or in any kind of uncertain condition, Carmen was my leader. Learning everything from the beginning was less intimidating because of her. I could depend on her to continue and keep the rest of the team together. Even when she was leading alongside a bigger male, she wasn't afraid to push him toward the right direction. She never turned around or lost focus, and she was smart about saving energy, resting at her house when there weren't any trips, never exerting the eager calls for attention that the rest of the pack did. I wanted her same composure, that ability to stay grounded when it felt like the whole Earth was shaking.

Everything I thought I knew about the world was lost. The storm was chewing on all of it: the mountains, the cabins, the mines, the sky. Carmen listened to the directions I gave her, but she was reluctant; she knew I doubted myself.

The day before, I had set up camp on top of an overlook in Hell's Valley, named for the red-orange color of the minerals melting from the mountainsides. I anchored the dogs in a circle around the tent to act as polar-bear guards, dug a toilet, started a fire, boiled water for the freeze-dried pasta. I tossed small blocks of meat to the dogs and they ate quickly, curled into balls with tails over their noses and slept.

That night, there had been a small sliver of light on the horizon and everything was washed in a deep indigo—"the blue hour," as the northerners call it. Before I went to sleep, I looked at the way the clouds swam overhead, the distant mountains brimming with snow threatening to slide, and I knew I was in a place that I could never truly understand, that it would always be a little bit out of reach—but if I tried hard enough at the right moment, my fingertips brushed against it. Witnessing power of that magnitude, is it awe or devastation that echoes through the heart?

After the whales disappeared, the fur trappers came north, first from Russia and then from Norway. They were men (and a small percentage of women) with dreams of the free life, of adventure and conquest in the wilderness. Most of them were after polar bear and fox fur, but when more people began overwintering, walrus and seal also gained interest. The landscape became a system of base stations and trapper cabins, and in order to be profitable the trappers had to catch as much as possible during ten to eleven months of the year. When the trappers returned to the mainland after their year on Svalbard, they were greeted not necessarily with economic wealth, but with social praise: they were regarded as heroes, as conquerors of the Arctic.

All over the Western world, people became taken with the idea of the north. What is it about this place that draws people in? Is it the space, the transformation, the shifting light? The physical manifestation of the unknown? The race to the North Pole began, and countless expeditions passed through, or tragically ended on, Svalbard.

With increased knowledge of the north, different countries began dreaming of ways to profit from the land. Coal mining began in the early twentieth century, although most often it wasn't lucrative due to the equipment expense and harsh conditions. With coal mining came settlements and cities, the division of land in order to lay claim to its resources. Svalbard had always been a no-man's land, an ungoverned place that anyone could use. Even after the Svalbard Treaty was signed in 1920, handing over sovereignty to Norway, Svalbard remained the Wild West of the Arctic—not its own country, but a mine: of imagination, desire, paradox.

Watch the way polar puppies experience the unknown. They're born in the cold, or in the dark—the midnight sun, if they're lucky. They fit in an outstretched palm, their fur sleek and thin, faces wrinkled, eyes tightly shut.

How they wake up: all at once. Suddenly, the world is in front of them. They learn how to leave the warmth of their house, how to wobble awkwardly on their newly discovered legs.

When I brought them outside their pen for the first time, the rest of the pack was howling at us, curious about what we were doing. The puppies were shy at first, standing up like it was the first time they had ever done it, but then something caught their eyes—a tuft of moss or reindeer fur—and once they stumbled forward they never stopped. Bravery was in their bones. They followed each other in a clump, bounding toward whatever strange thing happened to be in front of them, and this was how they found the world: waiting for them, endless. I watched them watching, how they were struck by anything, and it felt like learning to see again.

We had been going in the same direction for an hour when I saw it: the tall cabin that marked the far side of the valley, directly opposite from the yard. All we had to do was cross the few kilometers to the other side.

I shouted to Carmen to go left and she did, pulling the rest of the team with her. If we continued straight, we couldn't miss the yard. Eventually we would get to the road leading outside of town, and crossing that would bring us home. I thought I heard the low drone of snowmobiles in the distance, but they never materialized. Maybe we were the only living things left.

I hoped we would be lucky, that the storm would fade. I tried to imagine myself hours from that moment, outside of it. It was the part of every difficult journey where people try to bargain with unknown gods, as if nature cared about our sudden realizations of mortality.

The abandoned coal mine on the mountain above the dog yard had always been a beacon. As we continued, I looked for its faint illumination through the blowing snow. There was nothing.

Svalbard is scattered with deserted mining materials, whale-blubber boilers, broken fur traps and forgotten furniture. There's a Russian mining ghost town in a fjord north of Longyearbyen, often traveled through by polar bears looking for food.

Every year, countless human-made structures are destroyed by avalanches. Windstorms rummage through buildings. The polar night drains energy in a way that leaves everyone half asleep, lost in dream.

Nature continues, fiercely. The Arctic will never belong to anyone.

Shortly after I moved to Svalbard, a storm hit the valley where the dogs lived. Before the governor closed the road and evacuated part of town, I drove out to the yard with a couple of coworkers. We would spend the night there to make sure the dogs were safe.

It felt like the end of the world. The storm hadn't started yet, but the weather report said it would be bad. A bomb of anticipation had exploded and left a quiet layer of eeriness in its wake.

We spent the whole night chasing everything the wind threw

down—mostly doghouses, equipment. The shed holding all the sleds collapsed. It rained and rained. We made a fire inside the barracks and sat on reindeer hides, and whenever all the dogs started barking we went to check on them. They were made for those conditions; many of them were still outside their houses, wagging their tails and trying to play in thirty-meter-a-second wind. Carmen was sleeping outside, under her house. In the barracks, I drifted in and out of sleep and felt like the roof was going to fly off, like the windows would shatter.

"Let's go feel the weather," Trude, my coworker, said. We got in the truck, drove to the middle of the road and cut the engine. She told me she loved the north because of its power, the elemental forces that humans could never compete with. I thought she was right; maybe that's why this lifestyle had become so intriguing to me. There's something to be said about feeling powerless, about realizing the scale of how small we are.

When we climbed out to feel how strong the wind was, it was almost impossible to open the door. I remember standing outside and feeling like the gale could carry me, like if I let myself go I could just be gone.

The successful expeditions were the ones that merged with the landscape and forces that ruled it. Fridtjof Nansen built a ship designed to get stuck in pack ice, which would carry him farther north than any of his predecessors. There was no point in trying to subdue that which always continued.

Instinct wins. The dogs have a switch that flips and there's no shaking them from it; two dominant males fight to kill, a wandering reindeer will send some dogs into hunting mode, the pack tries to take out the weakest of their own. Times like those, a veil comes over their eyes and they disappear into their own nature. It once took three people to make one of the males release his hold on another dog's ear.

I searched for that level of boldness in myself: breaking up fights by pinning the dogs down and biting their ears; growling; rewarding good behavior through play and affection. It was a new way of speaking, a voice I had never used before.

In front of us, the same cabin we had passed fifteen minutes ago appeared again. We had gone in a big circle and not realized it. We were trapped in the belly of something.

We tried again. All we had to do was find the road. Carmen started pulling to the right on her own, and I stopped the sled to correct her. There wasn't enough snow for the anchor to hold, so I couldn't leave the sled to guide the team myself.

"Gå fram!" Go forward. She turned to look back at me with a stubborn gaze as if she was unimpressed, unfazed by this whole situation. She always had her own ideas, as any good leader does.

"Come on, Carmen, let's go," I told her. Still nothing—she

wasn't convinced. She kept trying to pull to the right.

I gave in and let her lead. To drive dogs is to yield to unpredictability, to at some point release control. She was the expert at navigation, even when there wasn't a trail in front of her. Sometimes it felt like she was the one training me.

People came north to make something known out of the unknown. The human mind wants to understand it all; it longs for knowledge or some glimmer of meaning. It wants to know the world, what's beyond the ice, when the storm will end. It wants to run and keep running.

The silence and noise of dogsledding: when the sleds and gang lines and harnesses come out, the dogs lose it. It's a cacophony of barking and crying and howling. They have only one desire: to go. They are impatient; they throw out a lifesaver and drag me to the surface.

And then: the release of the anchor, the release of sound. The sled goes flying forward whether you're on it or not, and the dogs are focused, mute except for the push of their paws through snow, the steady rhythm of their breath. Silence. Dog and landscape meet: bold, harmonious, complete. I feel the tension draining from all of us as we settle into the cadence of motion. We turn, alert, to the present moment.

Svalbard is a dream lost upon waking, the kind you startle from and feel but can't explain. We walk around with outstretched arms in the dark, looking for the right words; we come up empty-handed.

The first mention of Svalbard is in Old Norse historical documents, the Icelandic Annals of 1194, which state, "Svalbarðí fundinn—the land of the cold coasts has been found." There is no documented evidence of this journey, nor is there clarification on what the cold coast was; it could have been the edge of an island, the edge of pack ice, the edge of anything.

Even a year after her death, what I remember most about Carmen is her eyes. Bright, sharp and glacial blue, they almost seemed to mirror the landscape itself. She ran with the wind, and then she became it.

The sound came out of nowhere: howling, one drawn-out song between the dogs and the Earth. It was as if they were calling to us. Carmen was leading us toward the sound, and the whole team started running faster, sure of where they were going. The outline of the mine materialized, and then the small cabins surrounding it in the valley. The real world began there.

We were on the cold edge of something—somewhere between lost and found, between dog and human nature. All I had to do was hold on, watch the arched bodies of the team as they ran. We had made it, but I knew it wouldn't be the last time. There are hundreds of ways to get lost in the north, to get swallowed whole by the landscape. So many times, the dogs have pulled me forward; we run toward the brink of what we know, and we continue until there's only blank space, all the uncharted territory of mind and landscape merging, and then we work our way back home.

KELSEY CAMACHO *guides dogsledding trips in Longyearbyen, Svalbard, where she is also learning how to knit sweaters. Her nonfiction and poetry has appeared in* Proximity, Entropy, Coldnoon *and elsewhere. She was recently a writer in residence at Artica Svalbard, where she began writing an essay collection based on her experience in the Arctic.*

SEVILLA

BY KELSEY SWINTEK

RACCOONS, COMPLETE DESTRUCTION, ANDALUSIA, HICKEYS, STATUESQUE RESEMBLANCE, PINK CLOTHESPINS, TINDER INTERCAMBIO, SMALL PLASTIC HORSES, RUFFLED GOWNS, COPPERS, INFESTATION, INCOMPREHENSIBLE FINALES, TINTO DE VERANO & THE BOSS.

A narrow hallway with yellow walls. Canary yellow, like a ripe lemon or a taxicab. Faux-hardwood laminate flooring, rapping echoes from shoes at all hours. The kitchen, modern and clean. Shiny, candy-apple-red cabinets, barren. The bedroom windows overlook a lazy, serene courtyard. One large tree is visible outside amongst the nearby apartment buildings, a tree so remarkable that I wonder if it is older than the city itself. Four beds, one nightstand. I live here.

There are eighteen guest beds in the hostel, ten in one room and eight in another. Only one of the guest rooms is infested with bedbugs. Check-in for guests is from 9 a.m. to 2 a.m. Sheets cost an additional one euro. My boss is Joaquin. I found him online. He comes between 2 a.m. and 4 a.m., counts the money in the Ikea desk drawer and sends us volunteers a spattering of Facebook messages about HostelWorld reviews.

everything will be solve the day i build the website for rating HW customers via their email
so hostels can forsee bitching review in advance
its clean but people sucks

He wears red Puma sneakers, the same loose sweatpants every day and T-shirts with large holes in odd places, almost like he had been in a sword fight. He says he is a professor at the university, but I wonder if he teaches in the same clothes. Maybe? Joaquin is always "completely destroyed." Like, if you ask him how he's doing—"What's up? How was your day?"—the answer is always the same: "I am completely destroyed." I guess he means tired.

My first impression of Joaquin was from Facebook. He friended me after I replied to an ad he listed on WorkAway, a site for volunteers looking to exchange labor for accommodation. His Facebook name is Joa Quin, like it would be such a horrible breach of privacy if anyone knew his full name. He has one profile picture. His photo is cropped across the middle of his chin, eyes red from the flash, no bend of a smile, darkness behind him. Kind of like a raccoon you catch with a flashlight going through your garbage. Completely destroyed.

Three months after I graduate college, I'm working at my dentist's office. I hold spit cups for patients and sanitize metal tools. Joa Quin messages me the date that I could start work and some directions to the hostel from the bus station. I book a flight, and a bus. I forget to return my scrubs.

My bus arrives in Sevilla at 5:30 a.m. on a Tuesday. I'm the only person in the city who is awake. The duffle I filled with clothes and books and shampoo does not have wheels, nor straps to wear on my back. The two nylon handles dig into my bare shoulder and the weight of my life rests upon my hip. I hobble away from the only place I know in the sleeping city, the bus station. Joa Quin's directions omit words like "left" or "right." *Turn Calle Hernando Colón.* Metal cages protect the shop fronts. *Turn Menéndez Pelayo.* Names of streets are indicated in mosaic tile on the sides of the buildings. *Calle San José.* My eyesight poor. *You will see a church. Do not turn at the church.* Vines dangle from a canopy between the stucco apartments. I move toward the building, squint at the tile. *Plaza de los Curtidores.* A girl buzzes me in; we tiptoe toward the bedroom and she whispers inaudibly and points to an empty top bunk. Someone snores. I haul myself onto the mattress without brushing my teeth or going to pee or getting water, all things I yearned for during my labored journey. I sleep, without a blanket. The welcoming arms of the tree stretch toward me through the window.

The work schedule rotates every two weeks, so I work either forty hours or twenty hours. In addition to accommodation, I receive a stipend to cover my food: twenty-five euros for a forty-hour week, five euros for a twenty-hour week.

I strip the beds, collecting the white sheets in my arms, forming a pile so large I cannot see around it. I load the washing machine. I clean the men's bathroom. I half-ass try to clear the mold in the shower. Someone asks me for directions to Alcázar. I don't know. I point to the bulletin board across from the check-in desk at the door. I clean the women's bathroom. An orphanage of travel-sized bottles lies on the windowsill: abandoned L'Oréal, half-empty Neutrogena. The washing machine sings. I gather the damp white bundle into a plaid shopping bag and walk up the flight of stairs to the rooftop. A weathered wood table, some chairs. Laundry lines with pink clothespins. The leafy top of my tree spitting distance from where I stand. I spread the tangled sheets across the line, my fingers imbued with the scent of fabric softener. October sun tickles my pores. I go downstairs and sweep the laminate floors. I fill the red bucket with warm water. I mop the bedrooms, the kitchen, the living room, the yellow hallway. I wait, stranded at the check-in desk, until the floor dries. A guest emerges from a room, wordlessly crosses to the bathroom and shuts the door. I trace the trail of dirt footprints with my gaze, and I don't move. I just let it be.

I'm practicing my Spanish. That's what I tell people when they ask why I live in Spain. Tinder is the best way to connect with language partners, for *intercambio*. My Spanish isn't terrible, but the Andalusian dialect is terrible. Words are shortened and strung together, rhythmic emphasis completely different to what I'd learned in school, da-da-da-da-da-da, *vale*? The equivalent would be to move to Birmingham, Alabama, to practice the English you'd learned from a British teacher. My *intercambio* partners laugh at me, but patiently. All of the men I meet are as tall as I am, towering at five feet, five inches. Sometimes they hold my hand and sometimes they kiss my cheek. They buy me *cervezas*; we nibble on *croquetas* and olives. When I tell my friend at home about my *intercambio* partners, she laughs. She calls it something different: Tinder Food Stamps.

This is how I meet Novio. He does not have the typical dark Sevillano look. Novio is tall, with a shadow of a beard, light-brown waved hair and blue eyes. He does not speak English. At all. We drink *cervezas* and mime back and forth, laughing between broken syllables. When he holds my hand, he laces his fingers in mine so that the soft pockets of skin between our fingers are touching. We walk along the river and I ask him how to say "toes" and he tells me and I can't believe that such a cute English word is such a mouthful in translation.

We lay together in Plaza de España. Mosaic alcoves depict cities and villages of Andalusia. It is also a film site in *Star Wars*, but I don't know this until years later. Vendors lay knickknacks like small plastic horses and decorative flamenco fans on large blankets on the ground. They shout prices at passersby donning visors and camera straps. They shout at us: "One euro!" Novio leans toward me. "See? Now they think I'm a tourist because I'm with an American." He chuckles and playfully pokes my side. I'm disappointed that I will never fit in, but I don't tell him because I don't want him to laugh at me. We walk over to another garden within the park. Trellises woven with ivy and other flora surround a bronze bust and a couple of benches. The bust is tall, his fixed gaze staring right over the top of my head. His face is serious, frown lines prominent and brow bone pronounced. "This is my great-grandfather," Novio says. He has an odd sense of humor, but I laugh anyway. He points to the nameplate and I shut up. I look at Novio and I look at the bust, and I look back at Novio. The similarities emerge: thin, pursed lips, ears slightly out from the side of the head, round but strong chin. I never would have thought this bronze bust looks like Novio, but once I have this new information, my eyes shift focus, my brain playing tricks. I ask him why there is this bust, this ivy, this garden in his honor. He tells me a story, pausing sometimes to gauge my comprehension. *Vale?* I understand little of what he says, but I nod and smile anyway.

Nights that I don't have to work and that I don't see Novio, I walk. Moonlight beams a spotlight on the sleepy Spanish city. A man plays flamenco guitar each night near the cathedral. His cap likely conceals a balding head, and his faint laugh lines and crow's-feet are reminiscent of the gentle pencil marks of a blueprint. His guitar case lies ajar at his feet, the few coins bared under the yellow streetlight. Tourists hesitate as they pass him. Some pause, straggling behind a group to absorb the melody emanating from this strange man's fingertips. Standing, they tower above him. The man sits upon a stool, hunched over his instrument like Picasso's *The Old Guitarist*, dwarfed by the monumental cathedral. He never lifts his head, just nods gratefully at the click of more coppers tossed into his case.

I sit on the steps above the flamenco guitarist. I'm invisible. These concrete steps are an ideal reading spot. They are wide enough to perch comfortably, but not so wide that it is uncomfortable to lean back if I wish. They are well lit, and unlike a café or bar, I do not have to pay to sit here. I read. I hear the rhythm of the horses' hooves as they lead carriages back to the cathedral. The man takes a smoke break; the laughter of drunk students ricochets through the narrow streets and the horses march on. The melody continues, and it is only when he is packed up that I realize the music has stopped.

On my way home, men in orange jumpsuits hose down the winding deserted streets. I remove my sandals and splash about the cold puddles with my naked toes. They shut off their hoses while I pass. I wonder where the strange man with the guitar disappears to in the cracks of Sevilla.

When I wake up in the morning, I check my arms and legs for bites. The bedbug situation is dire. Guests approach me at the check-in desk, showing me swollen red marks on their arms, their backs, their legs. "Oh yeah, mosquitos are the worst," I say. A girl from Argentina brings me into the infested room. Her eyes are wide; I can tell she genuinely believes I do not already know. "See? These are all of the eggs." She traces her finger from the bed along the wall to the window. Small fuzzy gray dots look like dust, barely there but still visible to the naked eye. She wipes her finger across the trail of eggs, smears it across the white wall. I tell Joa Quin that the guests are starting to speak up; what should I do? *i cannot speak of this right now Kelsey i am completely destroyed.* I strip the beds and carry the mass of sheets as far from my chest as I can without seeming suspicious. I wash them at the hottest temperature because Joa Quin says this kills the bugs instantaneously. When the washing machine sings, I walk up to the rooftop with the wet bedding and hang it on the lines with the pink clothespins to dry in the sun.

Grocery List:
rice cakes
sweet potato
avocado
oats
eggs
carrots
apples
lentils
onion
zucchini

If I can afford it:
cheese
sliced turkey
tinto
pomegranate
pesto
alpro vanilla soy juice box cartons

Sometimes Novio picks me up in his little silver car. We drive and we talk. He drives me to the big grocery store so I can buy food. He drives me to empty parking lots so we can make out. He drives home because he has to use the toilet. "Wait here," he says. "Ten minutes." I nod and plug my phone in. I listen to "Hello" by Adele for ten minutes. I start to scream the words as I learn them. I'm crying in his little silver car. He comes back, tells me he has a surprise for me. He says it is a special date. He leans over the gearshift and kisses me as though it is the first reunion after we have been separated by a gruesome war for six years and I am his true love. He drives me to a lookout point outside of Sevilla. Windshield wipers screeching back and forth. We share an umbrella, look out at the yellow lights of the city as though through smudged glasses. The wetness of the night blurring and muting the light, but the cathedral, unmistakable, Gothic, grand. His arms around me, me holding the umbrella above us. *Hermosa*, no?

I'm hungover one day at a vegan café in Triana. When I finish my meal, I lie down and close my eyes. I'm hit by a truck. Not really, but that's how I feel, completely destroyed. I think I'm asleep; I hear a muted lullaby. *Hey little girl, is your daddy home? Did he go away and leave you all alone?* I perch up on my elbows and look around. Music of my people, music of my home. Bud Lights at the Jersey Shore in dive bars with loud amps and low AC. A man opening his wine stall hums along. *Tell me now, baby, is he good to you?* I dance I twirl I hop I smile I cry I sing. The man laughs and turns up the volume and at night I wake up with the sheets soaking wet and a freight train running through the middle of my head. The man cheers, "Bruce Springsteen!" I tell him I'm from the same place as Bruce Springsteen. I tell him my dad loves Bruce Springsteen. I tell him people play Bruce Springsteen at all of the bars in the summer, at the beach. I don't think he understands anything I say. "Home," I say. "This is home." He nods, comprehensively.

Our hostel advertises super-fast Wi-Fi. Joa Quin is paranoid that lazy people will uncover the password and use our super-fast Wi-Fi from the plaza below, slowing the connection for guests. For anyone in Sevilla in need of free, super-fast Wi-Fi, here is the password, as handwritten on paper on the informative bulletin board for guests:

Wi-Fi J
dashomoioiweltanschauung

The only rule of the hostel: No guests allowed. Joa Quin mentions something about how the hostel is not technically legal. Nobody from Sevilla is allowed to come to the hostel, or know where we work. Novio lives with his grandmother in Triana, and she is always home. One night, fingers entwined, we stumble through the alleys of Santa Cruz. We had a couple of carafes of red wine; he told me that I have beautiful eyes and I asked him if he enjoys to ride bikes. *¿Te gustas montar en bicicleta?* The cobblestones glisten, wet from an afternoon shower. The night is silent apart from the dull hum of traffic on the avenue, several blocks away. I'm the kind of drunk where my face is flushed and everything is hilarious. Novio's mouth is soft and wet and he lifts me so my legs are wrapped around his waist. He kisses my cheek and my neck and my chest and I look around and think how different the world looks from up here.

I bring him to the rooftop, with extra blankets from my room and one pillow for us to share. La Giralda pierces the black sky and my tree hushes in the breeze. It's chilly but my skin is hot from the wine. The weathered wood table collapses beneath us, and I think it's hilarious. Lying naked on a pile of crap, beneath the judgmental watch of the stars, Novio smiles. *Eres mi primera Americana.* You're my first American.

I tell Joa Quin that the Germans broke the table. *Focking Germans party idiots Nazi.*

There is a *churrería* around the corner. When the wind blows a certain way, I can smell it from my bedroom window. An old man spirals dough into the hot oil. I hear it sizzle and crack. I'm drooling. "Two euros, please." He wipes his fingers on his striped apron. Mostly copper coins spill from my hand to his. He places the churros in a paper case on the counter between us. *¿Azúcar?* I nod expressively. Sugar crystals rain onto the luscious dough. My first bite warms me to my center. I groan with pleasure. Eyes close. It tastes like indulgent relief. The inside of my mouth so wet, savoring every piece.

I find an open-air market one day, exploring a northern neighborhood of the city. I find vintage postcards on a table. I want to buy them, but when a fat man smoking a pipe tells me the price,

I cannot afford them. I find Feria posters, sketches of women in pink and orange and red ruffled gowns alongside a silhouette of La Giralda. I want to buy one, but I cannot afford it. I find a leather-bound notebook, the leather worn but the pages blank. I run my fingers along its spine. I want to buy it, but I cannot afford it. I find piles of books that I cannot read. I find an oversized fuchsia button-down shirt. There is a paint stain near the bottom, at the front. I cannot afford it. I buy it anyway.

Novio and I break up. I don't really know why. I thought he said that he wants me to come meet his family in his hometown, a mountain village a couple hours' drive. Maybe he said that he is going to see his family and he won't see me again. I'm not sad, but I'm kind of annoyed because I still have two weeks in Spain and I'm overdue for some groceries. That's a total lie. I cry so much, even Novio cries. I cry so much and I don't even know what he said to me.

Volunteers have the privilege to lock the bathroom door during slower hours. In the women's bathroom, there is just one latch lock on the main door. The toilet stall is private, and there are two semi-private showers and two sinks. To lock the door means to cut off access for guests to the toilet, showers, sinks and mirrors in the women's bathroom. When the guests go out to tourist, I grab my towel, my face mask and an orange Ikea mug of *tinto de verano*. I slide the latch across the wood frame. Daylight gushes through the windows. I play music, The National or Arctic Monkeys. I paint my face. I inspect myself in the mirror. Rogue hickeys left over from Novio or new moles on my back from the sun. The water pressure is weak but the warm water feels soothing on my skin. I ignore the knocks on the door.

KELSEY SWINTEK *is a writer and lover of daffodils. She graduated from the University of St Andrews with a degree in comparative literature and art history. She currently lives in a one-bedroom apartment with her best friend (and sometimes mice) in New York City. Find her on Instagram as @kelseypizza.*

HAT
PROTECTOR
די וואך
פורים
תשע"ט
180
SALT
Weinberger's
MATJES HERRING

A DAY IN CROWN HEIGHTS

BY PATRICIA STRIAR ROHNER

UNATHLETIC NECKS, SEGREGATED STUDENTS, FORTY-CENT BAGELS, STOCKING FEET, PALE PLAIN PINE, THE LUBAVITCHER REBBE, VELVET ENVELOPES, REDHEADED WIVES, SOLOMON'S MINE & ALL YOUR JUDAIC NEEDS.

The day is hot, touching one hundred, the first warm day after weeks of cold rain, and the men in their black garb, felt hats, side curls and unhealthy pallor mill in front of the yeshiva praying, talking and smoking, confronted by a hostile or indifferent outside world several blocks away where regular New York life goes on. Here in Crown Heights, the Jews, with their beards and fringes, go forward as they study and do *mitzvahs*, or good deeds, while their wives, in long skirts and sleeves and *sheitels* despite the heat, push their baby strollers and read from prayer books. As they stand on the meridian, the center part of the street across from the *yeshiva*, separated from the men, they try to inspire another soul to transcend its flaws.

The yeshiva is large and important, taking up a good part of the block, and inside the men and boys with thin, unathletic necks ponder and pore over huge books and worship in a vast hall, sitting, standing, rocking, *tefillin* wrapped around their head and arms, carrying their deep-blue velvet zippered envelopes with their *tallit* and books in plastic when they leave. Upstairs, the women, preparing for when they will raise large families and pass on the traditions, sit and study on wooden benches for visitors, hard as prison seats, the area smelling of disinfectant as a black woman mops the floor of the new bathroom. In this place the women can look down through a glass window and watch the men in their age-old rituals, customs and devotions.

Surrounding the yeshiva, the neighborhood Crown Heights stores are small and disheveled. The Crown Bagel shop has no waiter and only three wooden tables and a side counter where a sink with paper towels sits in the front window. People stand in line and order their breakfast specials for three dollars and fifty cents or bagels for forty cents apiece. The students come in with their black jackets and curly sideburns, their shirts sticking out of their pants, with their fringes hanging, and eat quickly so they can return to their studies. The young girls come before they go to school, also devoted to Jewish learning, and sit in long skirts eating bagels and cream cheese. Every few hours a man with beads of sweat on his brow emerges from behind the counter and wipes the tables clean and restocks the cooler. This is the only eating establishment in this Jewish area and it hums with business all day long. A hat shop, a bakery advertising kosher challah and cakes, small grocery stores with shelves of Gold's Borscht, Goodman's Macaroons and gefilte fish, a jewelry store named Solomon's Mine, an Israeli book shop announcing "All your Judaic needs," a liquor store, and gift shops with signs that the Messiah is coming.

Pictures of the founder of this Lubavitch sect, the Lubavitcher Rebbe, are scattered in the windows on the street.

However, it is at the yeshiva, at number 770, where the heart of Crown Heights lies. Here the long silver buses line up to take the little Jewish children to the Catskills for the summer. Here is where the Haredi have the same worries and petty jealousies as the rest, but try to reach past their human frailties. Here is where many of the men, rabbis and students congregate, and the women in the center of the street, on the grass with benches, wait for the imposing black hearse as it pulls up with the deceased body of a revered rabbi.

"He was a *tzaddik*," one woman says. "Helped the Russians. Never complained, even in his sickness. I've known the family for twenty years."

The back of the hearse is opened and the black-coated men gather around the casket, plain pine, simple, no ornaments, and kiss the pale wooden box, praying and rocking. The deceased rabbi had eleven children. Many are rabbis or studying to become one—one traveling from as far away as South Africa—and they stand at the back and sides of the hearse with their reddish beards and recite Hebrew words. The younger sons, leaner and fine boned, in black hats and sparse beards, bend their foreheads on the hearse's window and weep.

The hearse drives away with the black-frocked men walking behind. A contingent follows the body to Long Island, six miles away, to a vast Jewish cemetery, to bury the esteemed rabbi. At the cemetery the man who guarded the body during the night stands in a gray box because he is not allowed to mingle with the others. He is a holy man. The body must be interred quickly because the soul will suffer if it is not covered. The men carry the pine box to the site and lower it into the grave. The women stand back, separate, but the wife and daughters wail with the plaints of a storm through the heavy summer air over the gravestones, amidst the many gray monuments with Hebrew letters announcing the deaths of fathers, soldiers, husbands, grandmothers and great-grandmothers, all beloved, all departed.

The sons, the rabbis and the students begin to shovel the dirt on the pine box, rapidly, over and over again until the entire coffin is covered with the dark earth. The laments of the women continue, the red-haired women and the red-bearded sons all brokenhearted because their papa or husband is gone. Papers are passed, covered with Hebrew words, and everyone prays. Then the mourners remove their leather shoes, which someone puts in bags, and soft cloth shoes are distributed to the family members and the mourning period begins. After the men walk away, some in stocking feet because there were not enough soft-soled shoes, the mother and daughters proceed to the gravesite and say their goodbyes. Weeping, their golden-red heads bobbing and moaning, they reluctantly let the rabbi go to heaven, absent from their lives forever.

The men are instructed to leave the cemetery in one direction and women another. The sweltering summer heat and vast blue sky encircle the rows and rows of headstones, the black-coated men with their beards and prayer books, the women following. The family will sit *shiva* for seven days, wearing their ripped clothing and sitting in their home—mirrors covered—where they will hold a *minyan*, prayers held twice a day at 7 a.m. and 8 a.m., except on Saturday, the Shabbat, the Queen, when it will be held at 9:30 a.m. with at least ten men in attendance.

Special people, the ultra-orthodox, encased in the middle of New York, waking every day to the realization that the world isn't as they would like it to be, going forward, doing another mitzvah, inspiring another soul, praying to God, giving to charity, observing the Shabbat and believing that Jewish existence is a miracle. Crown Heights is a world of its own with its collective head held high.

PATRICIA STRIAR ROHNER *is a graduate of Brandeis University and has an MSW from Simmons University. She has published seven short stories, was a top-ten finalist in the Arts and Letters Contest and won honorable mention in The Masters Literary Award for Titan Press. Her work has appeared in* Flash Point!, Golda, New York Stories *and* True Story. *Her first novel,* Tzippy the Thief, *won first prize in the general fiction category at the Southeast Book Festival in 2016. She is currently writing her third novel and pursuing an MFA at Lesley University.*

HILLSIDES

BY SEAN CARROLL

For over a decade, my photographic explorations have focused on documenting the built environment and the cultural landscape of specific places. A resident of coastal flatlands for much of my life, I moved to Pittsburgh in 2016 and immediately became enamored with the unique topographical conditions of life in this verdant upland city. Situated within the lush Western Pennsylvania forest, on undulating terrain with a vista point from every bridge, hollow, hillside and street corner, Pittsburgh presents a unique case study for observing how we have built and inhabit urban space. Indeed, the land on which the city rests has forced this photographer to adopt new perspectives and methods of working. Consequently, I have embarked on making a collection of photos that examine the distinct features that make Pittsburgh a fascination by climbing city steps, peeking through the trees and bushes and approaching the cityscape from the angles that the terrain demands. In my explorations, I've gathered pictures that feature curious arrangements of the metropolis from above and below.

RAILROAD
CROSSING
2
STOP

DAVE -
I WENT
to THE HOSPITAL
FRANK
my BACK IS
KILLING ME

Holmes St

SEAN CARROLL *is an artist working in photography and video, raised in coastal Massachusetts, now living in Pittsburgh. His various projects have been shown in exhibitions throughout the U.S. and featured in* PDN, The Wall Street Journal, *the* New York Daily News, Fraction Magazine, Aint-Bad *and* Lint Roller, *among others. He received an MFA in photography from Pratt Institute in Brooklyn and currently teaches photography within the College of Fine Arts at Carnegie Mellon University.*

THE VINE OF LIFE

BY RUSSELL HELMS

(fiction)

PARROTS WITH BLUE CHEEKS, HARMONICAS, SUITED GENTLEMEN, FIDDLEHEADS, FANTASTIC LIGHTS, TAPIR BONES, GASOLINE, BACABA PALMS, CORN TORTILLAS, MAPACHO, *HURT, PEQUE-PEQUE ENGINES, AYAHUASCA & THE AMAZON.*

A man went brooding into the jungle. He stood as tall as a doorway and bumped his wide shoulders passing through them. He relished the wantonness of life, its uncertainties and shadows. He went in search of Mother Ayahuasca, the vine of life, to perturb the giddy demons painting smiles onto famines and hordes of locust. He liked lima beans cooked with butter and drove a small car that no one would be likely to steal.

In Peru, the jungle is vast and swallows its people, leaving it to the West and the East to give them names. But he had a name, Juniper, June for short. Random tattoos on his upper arms, a simple eye on his right palm, which he used to frighten his daughter and those of rigid faith.

His adventure began in Newark, New Jersey, thence to Iquitos, Peru, and up the Mighty River past Francisco de Orellana to places without names, without shadows. The river was deep, wide and brown, with an infinite stomach for gringos and unlucky natives. In the thirty-foot canoe with a peque-peque engine, he ate catfish roasted over coals, with always-ample rice. He was silent, the man guiding the boat buzzing like a bee in the Spanish of Iquitos and occasionally Yagua.

For four days the boat plied the Mighty River, a smell of green, brown and gasoline. Long trails of steam played with the towering canopy. They passed small islands in the river and spider monkeys chattering, stopping once to gather fresh water from a rushing stream fed by the daily rains. The man named June was hot by day and shivered by night, his blank mind anticipating the secrets of the vine, seeking power, protection and teaching.

Precisely at midnight, and with a lone rooster crowing in the distance, the moon full and dreadful, there was the light of a single candle on a crude pier made of poles. The driver muttered as if afraid and steered the boat toward the muddy shore, bumping the gnarled pier. With only a small pack containing a flashlight, a poncho and a few corn tortillas, the man named June stepped onto the pier, which floated on large water-soaked logs. He wondered if the boatman would stay, but determined for now to find the jungle father known as Don Aguirre.

He entered the dark tangle of trees, the moon's glow halted by towering Brazil nut trees and bacaba palms. The path was narrow and slick, and he wished for a machete. Ascending, he soon came to a clearing where collected were the bones of tapirs mixed with the bones of humans. On he walked, his sweat mingling with the tepid chill. He remembered the small book of forty pages, the map within, and watched for a sign and soon found it: a circular ruin of stones charred by fire.

For three days he waited, eating fiddleheads and the fruit of the pacay, which resembled a large green bean. On the night of the third day, Don Aguirre came, barefoot, dressed in white. He was a small man with a barrel chest and that solid belly that resists heavy blows. With him was an old woman bent with age, wearing a T-shirt and a skirt of motley cloth. Twisted into a bundle about her shoulders were the ingredients, the patched steel pot, a glass and sticks of wood from a sacred almond tree.

In broken Spanish they spoke and the man named June sat and leaned against a large stone, watching the sturdy woman craft a small fire and place within the pot the vine of life, *chacruna*, leaves of the deadly *toè* and a handful of powerful *mapacho*. The moon again was full but its light weak among the ruins. Unseen, parrots with blue cheeks whistled and popped, warning of the fall of darkness.

To prepare for the ceremony, the man named June disrobed and bathed in water floating with the petals of flowers of which he did not know the names. For a month now he had shunned oil, salt, sugar, spices, coffee and tea. The memory of recent events flooded over him. His daughter had been hurt by a man and a man was dead. Nothing would ever be the same. To the sound of a cymbal brushed with a palm frond, the man drank an elixir of Piñon Colorado, followed by three wooden cups of stale water. Seven times he vomited and Don Aguirre smiled.

The old woman tended the bubbling pot, stirring it with a carved stick in the likeness of an anaconda. She had unrolled a grass mat and placed around it stones of green that caught the faint moon. Upon this the man sat, waiting.

Don Aguirre pulled from his pocket an old harmonica and

with hardly any sound blew long slow notes that reminded the man of a steamboat from far away. Soon it was time, and from a bottle filled with palm liquor Don Aguirre drank and sprayed the man's head. Wiping the moisture from his eyes, the man called June felt strong and craved his lesson to come. The old woman brought the pot from the fire and filled a small glass halfway, handing it to Don Aguirre, who placed it on a small stone to cool. And Don Aguirre began to sing the first *icaro* of healing, of inner sight and of peace.

Perhaps a minute passed, perhaps an hour, and Don Aguirre's voice went silent. He motioned for the man to come, and he did, kneeling before the shaman. Don Aguirre took the glass filled with bitter and black. He lit a hand-rolled mapacho and blew smoke three times into the glass. "Sé fuerte," he said. Be strong.

The man called June took the glass with both hands and in a single move gulped the foul liquid, tasting like sour wine and dirt. His stomach rebelled, but he persisted and returned to his mat, lying on his back amid the ruins, the ancient fire. A great peace enveloped him and he imagined his daughter, his wife now passed. For half an hour the peace lingered like dew and then came fantastic lights. There was a large cartoon house, and there was flame in the basement. The fire rushed up the stairs with the face of a minor demon and consumed each floor but yet the house remained, blue, red, yellow. Don Aguirre sang. The old woman shook a handful of reeds.

The man called June stood at the top of an amphitheater, looking down, down, beyond the rows of suited gentlemen. In the center was a small man dressed in garb of yore with large hands crafting a human being bit by bit. His long arm reached and took a brain and then a kidney and then bones. The man called June knew what was about to happen and trembled as his heart was plucked, like thread being pulled from his chest, and placed into the forming man. Don Aguirre sang. The old woman shook a handful of reeds.

All that was lacking was a soul and some blood and there appeared a young lamb. Through a slit in the belly yet unclosed, the lamb entered, and the man's eyes opened, and after a moment he began to speak. He spoke of a labyrinth, of the nature of time and of a recipe familiar to the man named June. The creation stood and walked and June followed as if tethered like a balloon. For seven days and seven nights through clouds, lava, cotton and a vast plain littered with machines, the journey continued. When the journey was complete, June opened his eyes to bright sunlight. Don Aguirre and the old woman were gone.

He felt the scar on his chest and thought of his daughter. That surely she would have the answer, that surely she would know.

RUSSELL HELMS *has had stories in* Sand, Litro, Drunken Boat, Bewildering Stories *and other journals. He holds a lectureship in English at the University of Tennessee at Chattanooga. His novels are with Sij Books.*

Maker's Mark
WHISKY

IN A ROOM

BY KIM STRAVERS

CHEEKBONES, DIESEL, ROUGH SHEETS, UNSTEADINESS, LA-Z-BOYS, SHATTERED GLASS, BOURBON, DIRTY SNOW, THE FRATERNAL ORDER OF EAGLES, POSTCARDS, HOLLYWOOD ROMANCE, PRISONS & NORTH-CENTRAL OHIO.

It had been six months since we'd last seen one another. He'd traveled across oceans and continents without warning back in June, and contact had been disappointingly infrequent. But by December he was Stateside again, now settled in Cleveland. I was visiting family in Columbus; it was understood that we'd meet as quickly as possible. We just needed a rendezvous point, a halfway. My eyes moved across the map. Ashland. Maybe Burbank—a tribute; we'd first met in Los Angeles—or Congress, to say we had. I measured. "Mansfield," I wrote. He'd thought so too. "I'll reserve a hotel and send you the address. *Capisce?*"

This man had been a gust of sharp wind—swirling around, over and through me, penetrating to the marrow, leaving me gait-changed, goose-bumped, tangled. For a while there had been frenzy. When we were together, our words wound around one another like a caduceus. Our encounters were unmoored. Christ, they were unholy, even—genomic, his word. I could never get enough to last until the next time.

When he'd hopped a plane in early summer, it was supposed to be for a week. He was headed to his brother's wedding back East—Providence, I think it was. I knew somehow when he stepped off my porch that I wouldn't see him for a long time. I folded bare arms across my chest and watched him walk away.

Once, after our second or third time together, I'd laughed at my reflection in the bathroom mirror. A thick smear of mascara circled my eyes. He came in to investigate, still flushed and dizzy after sex.

"...but what if I like it?" he asked.

He leaned in, tipped my face toward his with both hands, and ran his tongue in a gentle line from cheekbone to brow.

Weeks passed and I hoped I could molt, let time whitewash me so I didn't feel so bolted to him. But the heart doesn't care about chronology. His near-silence was an unceremonious end to things, yet every time he volleyed a text, I went full teenager and lost my resolve to move on. What did the letting-go matter, I thought, now that we were going to be thrown at each other in a place neither of us had ever heard of?

I arrived first. It was about 9 p.m. on a Monday between

Christmas and New Year's. Downtown Mansfield was empty. Families had long finished dinner; the flicker of televisions synced with tree lights behind curtains. I circled back to the motor lodge on the southern edge of town. Across the way was a row of fast-food joints, cheap lodging and a Walmart. Dormant farmland sullied by dingy snow lined the highway. It was too cold to smell anything but diesel exhaust.

I drew the blackout curtains against the streetlights. Unpacked and sitting on the worn bed, I peeled the wax off a small bottle of Maker's Mark and sipped it from a Styrofoam cup. I was on my own tonight. He'd arrive the next morning. Eighty-nine bucks seemed like a fair price. I got the late-late checkout.

I've been in plenty of beige budget rooms like #114, and I fell into a familiar routine: turn the local news on. Unwrap a sliver of white soap in the bathroom. Lay out an over-starched towel by the bathtub. Finally I got into bed and kicked the sheets out of their hospital corners. Then I texted him and waited for what felt like a long time.

At 10:27 p.m., he wrote, "mm ill let you know when im close."

Sleep came slowly. I dreamed of dashed plans and woke at six. I wasn't hungry, but I tried a stale buffet croissant that hinted of plastic wrap. Most of it ended up in the trash. This smallish town felt vast now with the waiting. Outside with weak coffee, I lit a cigarette and scanned the commercial-industrial cluster down the hill. Tractor trailers beat a rhythm on the interchange.

Retirees pulled into Bob Evans for five-dollar biscuits and gravy. Commuters refueled at the BP and wiped exploded insects from their windshields. Bleak and transitory, the outskirts of Mansfield went about their anonymous and repetitive business.

It was hell waiting for him to pull up. The threadbare room was too small now, too hot. Apart from the Adultmart across the street on Interstate Circle and the Mexican cantina that shared the motel parking lot, there wasn't much to this outpost. It was a placeholder. When I heard two knocks and unlatched the deadbolt, though, Mansfield started to feel right-sized and well-placed.

There wasn't enough air in the room for either of us to speak, so we clutched and stared and traced until we kissed. The dusty spray of fake flowers beside the bureau mirror, the framed prints of ugly landscapes, the Leatherette ice bucket, the surprising La-Z-Boy were just right. We were in Mansfield, where we belonged.

The time together felt big, though there was much less of it than I'd wanted. Noon passed. The housekeeping cart rattled down the corridor. Incandescent bulbs glowed. The loam-colored coverlet slipped from the mattress. He dressed, then cracked the door open and left. The matter was settled. I waited until I couldn't hear his car anymore and stepped outside. Cold gray Ohio sunshine touched nondescript buildings, and hard gray asphalt froze my bare toes. Yes, I was in Mansfield, and no, you can't trust a map, now, can you?

Our arrangement was over; that was clear. But the trip wasn't. I wasn't done with it yet. Mansfield is a crumbling blip, a place I'd never visit again unless I ran out of gas. But there was a kind of holiness to it now, despite its shabbiness. Charm. Any town can be sacred.

I wanted a souvenir; I couldn't risk forgetting. If outsiders know of Mansfield, it's likely for one of two landmarks: the Ohio State Reformatory, because *The Shawshank Redemption* was filmed there, or Malabar Farm, now a state park, because that's where Bogie married Bacall one spring day in 1945. By now the town has settled back into its old ragged habits. I tried the prison even though I knew it was closed for the season.

I steered the rental south to downtown and through its narrow streets, looking for a gift shop or at least a place where I could get a decent coffee. I drove down Main Street, up Diamond, across Temple Court and Park Avenue. I passed City News (which doubles as Suzy's Smoke Room), the Little Buckeye Children's Museum, the Fraternal Order of Eagles. There's a sense of struggle against disrepair in Mansfield. Ohio winters are brutal. The frigid wind and sleet strip sidewalks of people and trees of leaves; folks brace every man-made thing along the road. It's a town built two hundred years ago on railroads and industry, and the abandoned forges and brick warehouses gape with broken panes. The gates came down on Fifth Street for a freight train, and I lowered the windows just to hear the whistle and chug.

I found what I needed, eventually. There was a postcard for sale at the wooden carousel in the middle of downtown, a simple black-and-white line drawing of the Reformatory. I knew as the register rang that I'd labor over the message, be careful with my handwriting, but that it'd stay stamped and undelivered. He is built to drift, fireproofed against attachment. His name is a place and his address is constantly changing, unannounced, as are all these shape-shifting places on my cartographic heart.

KIM STRAVERS *has spent much of her life immersed in adventure sports, writing and editing for outlets such as* ESPN, Surfer, Bike, META *and* The Golfer's Journal, *but was most recently published by* The Guardian. *In past lives, she's managed a beer and blues festival, co-founded a nonprofit and successfully wrangled a couple of political campaigns in a tiny mountain town. She is the managing editor of* Nowhere.

Nowhere Print Annual
2019

CONTRIBUTORS:
Jack Antal
Michael Boushee
Kelsey Camacho
Sean Carroll
Russell Helms
Patricia Striar Rohner
Kim Stravers
Kelsey Swintek
Marjory Woodfield

EDITOR: Porter Fox
MANAGING EDITOR: Kim Stravers
ART DIRECTOR: Sara Fox
DESIGN: David Knowles

ISBN: 978-0-578-49200-1

Many thanks to our supporters for making this issue possible:

AARON FINCH
AARON SIMON
ABBY BARBER
ABHILASH SARHADI
ADAM ACHRATI
ADAM BURKE
ADAM FOWLER
ADRIANA SANANES ZINGER
ADVENTURE CORPS
ALAN BERNHEIMER
ALAN RAYMOND
ALESSANDRA SANTO
ALLISON STICE BULKA
ALYSSA ROENICK
AMY BUCHANAN
AMY GORDON
AMY HARRINGTON
AMY HOLMAN
AMY REAMS
ANDREW UNRUH
ANNA BUTLER
ANNA MARTENS
ANYWHERE APPAREL
APRIL SOPKIN
ARIAN FINCH
AUSTIN BEEMAN
BARBARA SMITH
BEN NICHOLS
BERT ROTHKUGEL
BILL FINGLETON
BO DIXEN PEDERSEN
BOB RAMSAK
BOB READ
BRENT ANKLAM
BRETT SMITH
BRIAN BARRIS
BRIAN KNIGHT
BUDDY H.
CAITLIN FRY
CASEY CLINE
CATO VANDRARE
CC CHAPMAN
CHAD HANSON
CHIARA MININNI
CHRIS KAISER
CHRISTINE SHERMAN
CHRISTOPHER DALY
CHRISTOPHER FLAGG
CHRISTOPHER RESENDIZ
CHUCK SULLIVAN
CINDY GOLDBERGER
CLAUDIA TAYLOR
COLIN BANE
COLL WISE
COLLEEN KINDER
CONAL DARCY
COREY
CRYSTAL NOLAN
CYNTHIA LIEF
CYNTHIA STRAVERS
DANIEL OWENS
DANIELLA CLINTON
DAVE HOLTZ
DAVE MCLACHLAN
DAVID BETTENCOURT
DAVID BROWN
DAVID HUEBNER
DAVID L'HEUREUX
DAVID WHITE
DEBBIE CLARK
DENISE KHNG
DENNIS REED
DEREK LESLIE
DEVIN CLARKE
DIANA JOHNSON
DIANE SWINTEK
DION AGEE
DUNCAN M. MOWATT
DUSTIN MOLLO
EKATERINA HAZARD
ELIZABETH LASH
ELIZABETH MUNTEAN
ELLE ERIKSSON
EMILIA BURDITT
ERIC BRINK
ERIC SCHWARZKOPF
ERICA O'NEIL
ERIK T. JOHNSON
ERIN C. HUNTER
ETHAN BARTOLIC
FANNY IP
GABRIEL MARCUS SEOW
GAYLE EARLY
GIULIO GARAU
GRACE W.
GUS RANCATORE
HAPPY FRIDAY
HAYDEN MEEK
HEATHER KEARNEY
HEIDI VANDERLEE
HOLLY JO HACKETT
IAN CHUNG
IRENE SEIPT
IRIS EOM
ISAIAH WHISNER
ISIS MASOUD
J.P.
JACATRA
JACK BYERS
JACKIE BAKER
JAMES MCKELVEY
JAMES MOTT
JAMIE ZIOBRO
JAN DEMPSEY
JANINE PAPE
JASON ALLEY
JAYME
JEFF MORAN
JENELLE PIFER
JENN CASTRO SONG
JENNIFER COMEAU
JENNIFER LANDRUM
JEREMY HERTZIG
JEREMY MUSSON
JEROME POON
JESSE LOCKS
JILL GRAHEK
JILL MARIE HUBBARD
JILL PATTERSON
JIM CAPOBIANCO AND ACW
JOE OZANNE
JOHN EULER
JOHN M.
JOHN MARCH
JOHN STRAVERS
JOHN WAUTERS
JOSH STEINBAUER
JOSHIA MANGGALA
JOSHUA CHAPIN
JUAN SOTO
JULIA ANDERSON
JULIE CORMAN
KAREN BURNHAM

KAREN O'BRIEN
KASSIE KEENEY
KATE O'BRIEN
KATHLEEN OSBURN
KATHRYN MITCHELL
KATIE JACKSON
KATY DRAKE
KAY HENRY
KAYLEE EARLL
KEITH CARLSEN
KEITH REESTER
KIMBERLY IVY
KIMBERLY PIZZUTTI
KIMI CERIDON
KLAINIE NEDOROSCIK
KRISTIE DALY
KRISTIN SENEKER
KRISTINE DIETRICHE
LAURA ALEJANDRA
LAURA DENNIS
LEODIS SHARPE
LESLEY BRUNS
LESLIE CUYJET
LIBBY BELDEN
LIZ WILLIAMS
M. KULA
M. VILLACORTE
M.J. COREN
MAARTEN DELANGHE
MARGO VIERS
MARIANNE WORTHINGTON
MARJORIE MURRAY-URE
MARJORIE NESET
MARTHA CLARKSON
MARTIN KASTNER
MARY SCHEIBEL
MATT DAWSON
MATT HAYNES
MAY P. WEISS
MAYUR JAYARAO
MEGHAN B. MCGUIRE
MEGHAN TAKAHASHI
MEL ADAMS
MICAH DONAHUE
MICHAEL BARNSTIJN
MICHAEL J. SHYMANSKI
MICHAEL PAGE
MICHAEL WOLFE
MICHAEL ZWACK
MIKE COOPER
MONIQUE CHEUNG
NATE HART
NATHAN FAIRBANKS
NELLIE FOX SAVAGE
NICK WURM
NORB GARRETT
OLIVER HILL
OMAR HUSAIN
OSCAR SAUNDERS
PAM DUNCAN
PAMELA RAINEY LAWLER
PATRICK HOLLINGSWORTH
PAUL HAAHR
PAUL M. JACOBS
PEGGY SULLIVAN & ROD WILLIAMS
PETER TROLLOPE
PHYLLIS BELKIN
R. PINEDA
RACHEL VINCENT
RAY CARNS
RE WIKSTROM
REBECCA LARIVEE
REBECCA SANDOVAL
REGINA O'MELVENY
RICHARD CANINO
RICHARD ROSSI
ROBERT GILMAN
ROBERT WALKER
ROBIN REATH GRAVES
ROD MEARING
RONALD GRAVES
RONALD RAND
RORY MURPHY
ROSEMARY CAMOZZI
RYAN ERNST
S. PRIDE
SALLIE SHATZ
SAM MCGEE
SARAH COCHRAN
SARAH KAVOURAS
SCOTT GOODSTEIN
SCOTT MORRIS
SCOTT WIGGINS
SEAN
SEAN MCSPADDEN
SEAN RIVKIN
SERAH DELAINI
SERGE AVERY
SEUNG EUN CHUNG
SHARA KRONMAL
SINJIN EBERLE
STEPHEN D'AMICO
STEPHEN MILES
STEVE HAWK
STEVEN MOSCHIDIS
SUE FITZPATRICK
SUE LANGE & GARY M. CELIMA
SUMMER BRENNER
SUSAN ROETHER
SUSANNA FORREST
SYDNEY
TED CALLAHAN
TED SULLIVAN
TERRY STANUCH
THE LAMBY
THE NOGA PROJECT
THOMAS PUTNAM
THOMAS TILQUE
TOM ROBINSON
TONY CHAMPY
TRACY MICHELMORE
TRAVIS AUSTIN
TRAVIS TEETOR
VALERIE BACHARACH
VICKI WELBORN
WADE MCKOY
WANDA AASEN
WATSON K. BETTS
WILL ALDRICH
WILLIAM WEIR
XIA LI SUMMERFIELD

CPSIA information can be obtained
at www.ICGtesting.com
Printed in the USA
BVHW091206090419
545041BV00002B/2/P

9 780578 492001